Money, Money, Money!
Avoiding
the Lies of False
Prophets You Know!

Matthew Robert Payne

Please visit http://personal-prophecy-today.com to sow into Matthew's writing ministry, to request a personal prophecy or life coaching, or to contact him.

Cover designed by akira007 at fiverr.com.

Edited by Lisa Thompson at www.writebylisa.com. You can email Lisa at writebylisa@gmail.com for your editing needs.

The opinions expressed by the author are not necessarily those of Christian Book Publishing USA.

Published by Christian Book Publishing USA.

Christian Book Publishing USA is committed to excellence in the publishing industry. Book design Copyright © 2019 by Christian Book Publishing USA. All rights reserved.

Paperback ISBN: 13: 978-1-925845-13-6

Dedication

I want to dedicate this book to my scribe angel, Bethany, who inspires me and helps me write. She has become a great friend to me, and my writing would not be as good if she were not in my life.

Table of Contents

CHAPTER 1:

Avoiding the Deception of False Prophets and Teachers

I'd like to share a message today that has been a heavy burden on my heart. I hope with the Scriptures I've prepared that I'm ready to explain it. I hope that I do it justice and bring a message that is really helpful for you.

Jesus shared in Matthew 24 that, in the last days, many false prophets would arise and deceive many, even the elect, if that were possible. In other words, Jesus was saying that, in the very last days, false teachers and false prophets would arise and deceive a lot of people, even the set-apart ones, even the people on the narrow way who are the very elect.

When Elijah ran from Jezebel and hid in a cave in fear of his life, he was pouring out his heart to God in depression, saying, "Take me. I don't want to live anymore." God told him that he had seven thousand in Israel who hadn't bowed their knees to Baal. He was saying, "Elijah, you are not the only one." Elijah thought he was the only one, but seven thousand other people, the elect of God, were still following God.

It's pretty concerning that even the elect, the set-apart ones of God, could be deceived. Since Jesus shares that warning in Matthew 24, a lot of people wonder the following:

- Who is a false prophet?
- How do I discern a false prophet?
- Am I being influenced by a false prophet?

- Is the false prophet someone who claims to be a prophet?

Many people in certain denominations, such as Baptist churches, believe the gifts ended with the last of Jesus's apostles. They believe that anyone who claims to be a modern prophet is a false prophet. That teaching is wrong because there are true prophets. They're wrong about that.

Many people from those sorts of camps really attack modern-day prophets and preachers. Anyone who disagrees with their teaching or what they believe the Bible says is a false teacher and a false prophet.

I grew up in a Baptist church; later I became Pentecostal. I would say I'm in the middle of the road now. I can speak in tongues but not very well. I have given about twenty thousand personal prophecies in my life. I would say I'm quite experienced at delivering personal prophecies that have proven to be accurate many times.

I want to start this passage with the last part of the Sermon on the Mount. Some teachers say that the Sermon on the Mount in Matthew 5–7 isn't relevant for today. People preach that you can't live the life Jesus called you to in the Sermon on the Mount. Modern preachers today say the preaching of Jesus doesn't have to be obeyed. Hyper-grace teachers and extreme greasy-grace preachers say that we don't have to obey the teachings of Jesus today. This is false teaching. I'm going to read some of the words of Jesus and then explain a little as we go verse by verse for further understanding.

In Matthew 7:13–28, the first heading in the *New King James Bible* is "The Narrow Way."[1]

"Enter by the narrow gate; for wide is the gate and broad is the way that leads to destruction, and there are many who go in by it. Because narrow is the gate and difficult is the way which leads to life, and there are few who find it" (Matthew 7:13–14).

Many people who haven't researched the Word much or who aren't intimate with Jesus would look at that passage and think that the people of the world go by the broad way. And they think that the narrow gate and the difficult way and the few who find it refer to life when you become a Christian.

I disagree with that view, and I feel that Jesus disagrees with it, too, even though it's preached by popular preachers. I believe that Jesus was preaching to the people who wanted to listen to him. He wasn't preaching to the world. He was preaching to those who came out to listen to him. That's different than preaching on TV, which goes out to a whole lot of people who are non-Christians. He was preaching to the people who wanted to learn from him.

The truth of the matter is the Christian church, the people who go to church, is the broad way. Many people sitting in church, if they died tonight, wouldn't end up in heaven. That is a shocking and sad statement if I am right. Many people who have said a sinner's prayer were sitting in church practicing sin and not repentant from sin, not even knowing they're sinning, and they're on a broad way that leads to destruction.

Only a few Christians follow Jesus and everything he taught. That way is difficult, and few find it. What is this path: this narrow path, this difficult path, this path that few people find? Well, Jesus said, "If anyone wants to follow after me, he must deny himself, take up his cross, and follow me" (Matthew 16:24, author's paraphrase).

I have a short book that was released earlier this year (in 2019) that explained, "Deny yourself, take up your cross, and follow me." You can find my book, *Do We Do What Jesus Said?* on Amazon. But the Christian life is preached by many who think you can have the best of the world and have Jesus too. But Jesus said, "No one can serve two masters; for either he will hate the one and love the other, or else he will be loyal to the one and despise the other. You cannot serve God and mammon" (Matthew 6:24).

The modern teachers, the false teachers, will teach that you can have wealth and abundance and you can have Jesus, too, and it won't cause any conflict in your life. Jesus taught against this. Of course, there can be wealthy Christians. There can be wealthy people who are totally in the will of God. I'm not saying there aren't. I'm just saying it's hard to be in that position. It's hard to live a life with a lot of cash going through your hands without being carnal, without loving the world, and without loving the lust of the world.

We'll go on. Matthew 7:15–20 says, "Beware of false prophets, who come to you in sheep's clothing, but inwardly they are ravenous wolves. You will know them by their fruits. Do men gather grapes from thornbushes or figs from thistles? Even so, every good tree bears good fruit, but a bad tree bears bad fruit. A good tree cannot bear bad fruit, nor can a bad tree bear good fruit. Every tree that does not bear good fruit is cut down and thrown into the fire. Therefore by their fruits you will know them."

Well, people don't usually know false prophets and teachers by their fruits. They don't understand what true fruit is. Jesus said in verse 19, "Every tree that does not bear fruit is cut down and thrown into the fire." If you're not bearing fruit, you'll be cut down and thrown into hell. Jesus is saying that about not only the false teachers but also about all those who follow them and don't bear fruit.

What is bearing fruit? Bearing fruit is doing the good works of the kingdom, saving souls, feeding the hungry, and increasing the kingdom of God on earth. These false prophets appear as Christians in sheep's clothing. They appear as sheep, but they're ravenous wolves.

What are wolves? Wolves hunt and travel in packs. False prophets and false teachers don't necessarily travel alone. They have many comrades and people who will write lovely endorsements for their books. These are well-respected, well-known names that are teaching heresy, that are teaching false words. These are not only well-known false teachers and false prophets but well-known people who write the endorsements for their books.

They're ravenous wolves. They're hungry. What are they after? Well, they're after people to follow them. They build up their own kingdom. They sometimes seem to have a cult following. They are after money. Many times, they are after money.

Someone who says, "Give to me and you'll get a thirty or sixty or hundredfold return," is using a Scripture in the Bible and making it say things that it doesn't say. If you listen to teachers who preach a message and then say give to them to receive a thirty, sixty, and a hundredfold return, why don't those teachers give a million dollars and receive a $100 million back? Then they wouldn't have to ask anyone else for money again.

What about those teachers who have $20 million houses and jets? Why don't they give away a million dollars a month and get a $100 million back each month? They would never have to ask again and could give some great ministries a million dollars. They could sow a million dollars and receive their hundredfold return every month, which would always come back to them as $100 million. They could then sow another million dollars. Truly if that really worked, they would not need to preach it so often. Everyone would be doing it.

I'm not saying that sowing and reaping doesn't work. You didn't hear that from me. Once I sponsored a Christian ministry called Revival or Riots. They were writing some quality material, and I really loved their teaching. The Lord impressed on me to start to support them. I started to give $30 a month. The first month, I gave $30. Other people then gave me $300 in gifts and cash. The second month, I gave him $30 again; I received another $300. The third month, I gave another $30 and received yet another $300.

By the fourth month, the ministry had fallen into universalism (the teaching that says that everyone—even Satan and his demons—will be saved). I've been deceived by this in the past, so I stopped giving to that ministry. I didn't want to support preaching error. But for three months, I was receiving a tenfold return on my money.

It is possible to receive a tenfold return. But many times, people ask you to sow into them, and they appeal to your greed. These false prophets and false teachers are teaching a prosperity doctrine that simply doesn't work in Africa or in other third-world nations. If it doesn't work in Africa and India, it's not true. Only real truth works all around the world.

You'll know them by their fruit. Fruit is sometimes hard for people to discern.

When Jesus said, "I never knew you," that was an example. "Not everyone who says to Me, 'Lord, Lord,' shall enter the kingdom of heaven, but he who does the will of My Father in heaven. Many will say to Me in that day, 'Lord, Lord, have we not prophesied in Your name, cast out demons in Your name, and done many wonders in Your name?' And then I will declare to them, 'I never knew you; depart from Me, you who practice lawlessness!'" (Matthew 7:21–23).

We have a few things to unpack in this passage. Some say that these people weren't Christians. People who believe the doctrine of once saved, always saved, which is a false teaching, often say that the people referenced in this passage are not saved. But people who believe that can't accept that Christians would be sent to hell. That's against their theology. They can't therefore interpret these verses to mean that these people are Christians. This verse baffled me for close to twenty years until last month.

One thing stands out here. Non-Christians don't call the Lord Jesus "Lord." Someone who thinks Jesus is their Lord calls him "Lord." Jesus said once in his teaching, "Why do you call me, 'Lord, Lord,' and do not do what I say?" (Luke 6:46 NIV). People who do what Jesus says are doing the will of the Father in heaven. These people do what Jesus taught with their life. Jesus said in John 14:21, "He who loves me obeys my commands" (author's paraphrase).

Non-Christians would not say Lord, Lord in that day. They wouldn't even expect to be saved. Non-Christians know that they've rejected Christ. They wouldn't be coming to Jesus, saying Lord, Lord. These are people who were Christians, had the anointing of Christians, and are coming to the Lord and appealing to him because they are being led off with the goats toward hell. "Many will say to Me in that day, 'Lord, Lord, have we not prophesied in Your name, cast out demons in Your name, and done many wonders in Your name?'" (Matthew 7:22).

One normally prophesies through and with the Spirit of God. But I have said things in prophecy that weren't true, and the people knew it wasn't true and that it came from my flesh. I've given prophecies that came from a spirit of Satan or a demon. I've given false prophecies and prophecies that weren't true. But the majority of prophecies I've done have been done by the Spirit of the Lord. I know they are true because I tell people about their life and give them accurate details that I couldn't possibly know aside from the Lord.

These people in this passage have said to Jesus, "We've prophesied in your name," which means they are prophets. Remember, the passage above was talking about false prophets. False prophets are true prophets who have just been caught up with a major sin in their lives. I will build a theme in this teaching on covetousness, the love of money, the love of riches, and the love of wealth.

A false prophet could be a person building their own empire for popularity or financial gain. They can prophesy. They have the Spirit of God. They can prophesy accurately. They can minister and cast out demons with the anointing of God. They have the power.

Remember, non-Christians can't cast out demons. Certain witch doctors can transfer demons and take a demon from here and put another demon in, but they don't really deliver people. Remember the story in Acts 19:11–20 when the sons of Sceva tried to deliver a person. The demon said, "Paul, we know. Jesus, we know, but who are you?" They attacked the men, and the men trying to do the deliverance ran out, stripped of their clothes and naked. That's what happens to non-Christians when they try to deliver people from demons.

They prophesied in Jesus's name. They had the anointing to cast out demons and had done many wonders in Jesus's name. A false prophet, someone who's anointed by God, but practicing a sin that is grievous to the point of costing their eternal salvation, can do signs and wonders with the power and the Spirit of God.

The Spirit of God can do the following through a false prophet: prophesy, cast out demons, and do signs and wonders. Some might say that's crazy. Well, it is! That is crazy. That's why so many people are deceived because these false prophets look like sheep. They look like the true vine.

Jesus says, "And then I will declare to them, 'I never knew you; depart from Me, you who practice lawlessness!'" (Matthew 7:23). "I never knew you" is the wording for intimacy in the Old Testament. Genesis 4:1 says that Adam knew Eve and bore a son. The word "knew" in that context in Genesis meant sexual intimacy.[2] When Jesus says, "I never knew you," it's a sign of personal intimacy with him.

If you're truly close to Jesus, you won't be covetous. You won't desire to make a whole lot of money from the gospel. As fast as the money comes into your ministry, it will go out on things of the ministry, not on new clothes, new cars, Rolex watches, and BMWs. Those who practice lawlessness or iniquity or who are unrepentant know that they are wrong.

Sadly, many of these false prophets believe in their own prosperity doctrine. They have been deceived themselves. They believe that you can make millions of dollars a year off the gospel. They believe it's a great way to make money. They believe they're going to heaven because they're prophesying, casting out demons, doing signs and wonders, and healing people. They believe they are right and that they are in this great place with God right up until the day they die, and then they find out that it's a different story.

How do we avoid this? Well, we need to travel the narrow way, which is how we started. What's the narrow way? The next heading in *The New King James Version* is "Build on the Rock."3

"Therefore whoever hears these sayings of Mine, and does them, I will liken him to a wise man who built his house on the rock: and the rain descended, the floods came, and the winds blew and beat on that house; and it did not fall, for it was founded on the rock.

"But everyone who hears these sayings of Mine, and does not do them, will be like a foolish man who built his house on the sand: and the rain descended, the floods came, and the winds blew and beat on that house; and it fell. And great was its fall."

And so it was, when Jesus had ended these sayings, that the people were astonished at His teaching, for He taught them as one having authority, and not as the scribes (Matthew 7:24–29).

Now what are these sayings that he's talking about? The passage refers to a wise man who built his house upon the rock or "these sayings." What does Jesus mean? Well, it's everything he said in Matthew 5–7. If you really want to understand what he meant, you can look up "The Fifty Commands of Jesus" on Google and find the Ezine article that I wrote.4

Jesus gave fifty commands, things he said to do and not to do. These are his sayings, his commandments. To paraphrase the passage about the wise man who built his house upon the rock, Jesus says, "A wise man is the person who knows my commandments and practices my commandments." That's the narrow way. That's the hard way. That's the difficult way that leads to life. If you practice those, you'll be safe. No false teacher can lead you astray because any false teacher would be coming against what Jesus taught.

But you're a foolish builder if you sit in church all your life and don't understand what Jesus taught, and therefore you're not practicing it. In that way, you can be open to deception because you don't understand the truth.

Certain hyper-grace teachers teach that the gospel didn't really start until Jesus was resurrected. Some of them say that Jesus was preaching the law on steroids. In other words, Jesus was preaching an amped-up law that was impossible to obey. They tell themselves and those they teach that they won't even try because he was teaching something impossible to do. They say that we're not even going to do it. We're going to make up a doctrine, a false doctrine, that says you don't have to obey Jesus.

Jesus was clearly saying that that's the work of a foolish builder who builds on the sand. Jesus was clearly saying that only the wise builders hear what he taught and practice it. Jesus said very clearly that those who teach others to not obey his commands will be called least in the kingdom of God.

Do you want to avoid being led astray? If you want to be on that narrow path that leads to life, obey Jesus. Find out what he taught. Look up the teaching, "The Fifty Commands of Jesus,"5 on Google. Look up my article and obey what's in it. Print it out. Put it on your fridge and start to obey it.

False teachers and false prophets could deal with many major sins, but I'm going to pick on one. I'm going to pick on one type of sin, and we'll have a deeper look at that sin. We'll look at some of the fruit of a false prophet and a false teacher. Bear with me as I go through some more verses.

Colossians 3:4–6 says, "When Christ who is our life appears, then you also will appear with Him in glory. Therefore put to death your members which are on the earth: fornication, uncleanness, passion, evil desire, and covetousness, which is idolatry. Because of these things the wrath of God is coming upon the sons of disobedience."

Who are the sons of disobedience? The people who practice fornication, uncleanliness, passion, evil desire, covetousness, and idolatry. You wouldn't want one of these sons of disobedience teaching you, would you? The wrath of God is coming upon these sons of disobedience. You wouldn't want one of them running your church or writing the books that you read or preaching the sermons that you follow on YouTube, would you? You wouldn't want one of them as a leader.

Many people are sons of disobedience. I could really name some names here, but I'm not going to do that. I'm just going to point them out to you now based on their actions. One of those sins is covetousness, which the passage goes onto say is idolatry. Idolatry is putting something else in the place of God or making an idol of money.

Isaiah says, "These men are foolish. They cut up half of a block of wood and make a fire with it. With the other half a block of wood, they carve an idol and worship it" (Isaiah 44:15–17, author's paraphrase). These people are crazy.

We look at idolatry and think that's for Eastern religions bowing down to idols of Buddha and all sorts of gods. It's not just for them; we're idolaters too. We're idol worshippers. Until recently, money was made out of paper, which is made from wood. We burn our fires with wood and generate electricity through coal and burning things. We make half of our wood into money, which we bow down to and worship.

The sin of idolatry is rampant in the Christian church. So many people are affected by it. I personally believe that more than half of the people attending church are lukewarm. I don't have specific statistics to back that up, but that is my perspective, based on what I've seen throughout the years. If Jesus came tonight, these people wouldn't go to heaven. If you feel that you might be lukewarm, it's time to turn around, repent, walk the other way, and start to act differently.

The false prophets are all about getting rich, all about you getting rich. The say that the way you get rich is to give them money and then God will give money to you. That's their message.

They also preach that you can be unclean. They also teach that you can sin and that God forgives you, that you're free. For instance, some of these hyper-grace teachers will teach that you don't need to repent. You only need to repent when you become a Christian, and then you don't have to continue to repent. But 1 John 1:9 says, "If we confess our sins, He is faithful and just to forgive us our sins and to cleanse us from all unrighteousness." The hyper-grace teachers say that's only for a person who is being saved and not for Christians today. They put a spin on everything.

Their fruit is that they are into money and possessions. They're covetous; they practice covetousness. God emphasizes that sin in 1 Thessalonians 2:4–6, "But as we have been approved by God to be entrusted with the gospel, even so we speak, not as pleasing men, but God who tests our hearts. For neither at any time did we use flattering words, as you know, nor a cloak for covetousness—God is witness. Nor did we seek glory from men, either from you or from others, when we might have made demands as apostles of Christ."

In this passage Paul is saying, "We didn't use flattering words. We didn't build you up and puff you up and say, you are so wonderful. We didn't use those flattering words as a cloak for covetousness. We didn't build you up and say that you are sons of the king. We didn't say that you deserve to live like a king. We didn't praise you. We didn't tell you that you deserve to be rich, healthy, wealthy, and wise. We didn't tell you that we love you so much, and you should give us all your money, and God's going to bless you."

Paul didn't do that. "We didn't seek the glory of men," Paul says. Many of these false prophets and teachers like to build a platform for themselves. They like to build a name for themselves and have a large following. They put out a book that becomes a best seller for a while until book sales die down as a normal course of matters. With more than fifty books out, I know how the pattern goes. They're popular for the first couple of months. Then the sales start to drop.

Paul didn't seek glory from men. False prophets will have you praise them and give them glory and take the glory of the Lord and then press you for money.

First Timothy 3:2–5 says, "A bishop then must be blameless, the husband of one wife, temperate, sober-minded, of good behavior, hospitable, able to teach; not given to wine, not violent, not greedy for money, but gentle, not quarrelsome, not covetous; one who rules his own house well, having his children in submission with all reverence (for if a man does not know how to rule his own house, how will he take care of the church of God?)"

Paul focuses on three things here: not greedy for money, not covetous, and not quarrelsome. Many men of God—wolves in sheep's clothing—have $20 million houses and $250,000 cars, $10,000 suits and $60,000 gold Rolex watches on their arms. They are greedy for money, peddling the gospel as a way to earn a living, not as a way to bless people. But they are covetous in all their ways, seeking after the world's goods, keeping up with the Jones's, and living a lavish lifestyle. That's another sign of a false prophet.

Hebrews 13:5 says, "Let your conduct be without covetousness; be content with such things as you have. For He Himself has said, 'I will never leave you nor forsake you.'"

Here is Paul in Hebrews. "Let your conduct be without covetousness. Be content with such things that you have." That's the key to overcoming covetousness in your life. Be content with the things that you have.

Turn off the advertisements on TV. Stop reading the advertisements that compel you to go after the things of the world, to go after the latest brand, the latest technology, the latest invention, the latest fad, the latest this, the latest that, that has you continually spending. Be content with what you have.

Use a computer until it's too old to operate. Then get yourself a new computer. Don't upgrade your computer every year. You don't need to upgrade your iPhone every year. Just upgrade when your plan runs out. You can have an iPhone for four or five years, and it will still operate fine.

Be content with what you have. I hope this is speaking to you because the false teachers and the deceived all go to hell. The false teachers and all the people they deceive go to hell.

This is why it's so important not to be deceived. This is why it's so important to travel the narrow way, to live the narrow way.

The first heading in the *New King James Version* for 2 Peter 2:1–9 is "Destructive Doctrines."[6]

But there were also false prophets among the people, even as there will be false teachers among you, that will secretly bring in destructive heresies, even denying the Lord who bought them, and bring on themselves swift destruction. But there were also false prophets among the people, even as there will be false teachers among you, who will secretly bring in destructive heresies, even denying the Lord who bought them, and bring on themselves swift destruction. And many will follow their destructive ways, because of whom the way of truth will be blasphemed. By covetousness they will exploit you with deceptive words; for a long time their judgment has not been idle, and their destruction does not slumber.

For if God did not spare the angels who sinned, but cast them down to hell and delivered them into chains of darkness, to be reserved for judgment; and did not spare the ancient world, but saved Noah, one of eight people, a preacher of righteousness, bringing in the flood on the world of the ungodly; and turning the cities of Sodom and Gomorrah into ashes, condemned them to destruction, making them an example to those who afterward would live ungodly; and delivered righteous Lot, who was oppressed by the filthy conduct of the wicked (for that righteous man, dwelling among them, tormented his righteous soul from day to day by seeing and hearing their lawless deeds)—then the Lord knows how to deliver the godly out of temptations and to reserve the unjust under punishment for the day of judgment.

Heresy teaches something that contradicts the Scriptures. Heresy goes against the Bible and is not scripturally sound. Hyper-grace and prosperity-doctrine Scriptures look as if they support these teachings if you take them out of context. But they even deny the Lord that brought them and now bring swift destruction. How much more could you deny the Lord Jesus when you say you don't have to obey anything Jesus taught? Jesus, they say, was teaching the law on steroids.

They teach that the gospel didn't come until Jesus was resurrected. Therefore, they say that you don't have to obey what Jesus taught because Jesus was teaching an amped-up law, so you don't have to obey him. They're denying the Lord.

Jesus said in this passage that he's not going to judge anyone in the last day, but his word will judge them. What if you lived your whole Christian life believing that lie that you don't have to obey Jesus, and then when you die, you find out that you had to obey Jesus to get to heaven? Remember the passage in Matthew 7 when Jesus said the wise builder built upon and obeyed his words. He said the foolish builder disregarded his words.

Many people follow prosperity-doctrine preachers. Many people follow the hyper-grace, greasy-grace platform. Many people are deceived.

"By covetousness they will exploit you with deceptive words; for a long time their judgment has not been idle, and their destruction does not slumber" (verse 3).

They'll deceive you, promising you a healthy, wealthy, rich, wise, prosperous life.

I don't have much money, but I am prosperous. I spent $46,000 last year producing books that cost people ninety-nine cents to buy. To be prosperous is to have enough money to do the will of God and having enough money to share with others, plus provide for your own needs. I only bought things for myself with about 2 percent of the $46,000. And even 2 percent is probably too high of an estimate.

These false prophets will teach you to deny Jesus and his teachings. They'll teach you to live in the world, love the world, and go after all the things of the world. They'll teach you that if you give to them, you'll get money from God, and everyone can be rich and happy. These are the kinds of things they teach.

If you're being taught these types of things from certain teachers you know, get rid of those teachings. The next heading in the *New Kings James Version* is "Doom of the False Teachers."[7]

"For if God did not spare the angels who sinned, but cast them down to hell and delivered them into chains of darkness, to be reserved for judgment; and did not spare the ancient world, but saved Noah . . ." (verses 4–5).

Peter says that God cast them down into hell and delivered them into chains of darkness. Some of these hyper-grace teachers teach that there is no hell and that you won't be judged. They teach that everyone will be saved and that there's no eternal punishment. They say and preach that a God of love wouldn't send anyone to hell.

"And did not spare the ancient world, but saved Noah, one of eight people, a preacher of righteousness, bringing in the flood on the world of the ungodly; and turning the cities of Sodom and Gomorrah into ashes, condemned them to destruction, making them an example to those who afterward would live ungodly" (verses 5–6). This refers to men having sex with men and women having sex with women.

When angels came to town in Sodom, the men of the town wanted to rape the angels. The angels had to strike everyone blind to stop that from happening. "And delivered righteous Lot, who was oppressed by the filthy conduct of the wicked (for that righteous man, dwelling among them, tormented his righteous soul from day to day by seeing and hearing their lawless deeds)—then the Lord knows how to deliver the godly out of temptations and to reserve the unjust under punishment for the day of judgment" (verses 7–9).

God knows how he's going to judge the false prophets and false teachers. He's going to judge them. They're going to go to hell even though they're anointed, can prophesy, can cast out demons, and can do signs and wonders. Even though they can do all that, even though in our eyes, they are true Christians, they're doing it for money, and their god is their belly.

He knows how to deliver you because you're reading a book based on this. He knows how to deliver you also. God knows how to judge sin. I hope this is making sense to you, and I hope you're thinking of certain teachers that you've been listening to. You might want to turn off their recordings and get rid of their books. This book came from a series of videos that I did. Many names of well-known preachers came to mind. But I promised myself I would never name names if I was ever to do a book like this.

The next heading is "Depravity of False Teachers."[8] "But these, like natural brute beasts made to be caught and destroyed, speak evil of the things they do not understand, and will utterly perish in their own corruption" (2 Peter 2:12).

They speak evil. They condemn the teachings of Jesus. They speak evil of them. They say that the gospel was not active until the resurrection of Jesus.

Just a side note, after Jesus was resurrected, after being back for forty days, he gave the Great Commission, which is after the resurrection, so that's when the gospel started. They didn't move the instructions of Jesus far enough into the future because they forgot that this verse was spoken after Jesus's resurrection. When Jesus was ascending, he gave the Great Commission, and he said in that teaching, "Go into the world and save the lost and teach them everything that I commanded you" (Matthew 28:19–20, author's paraphrase). That was after the resurrection. Jesus said, "Teaching them to do everything that I commanded you," so Jesus really did mean for us to practice what he taught.

"They speak of evil of things they do not understand or utterly perish in their corruption" (2 Peter 2:12, author's paraphrase).

The enemy doesn't like it when I read this Scripture.

"And will receive the wages of unrighteousness, as those who count it pleasure to carouse in the daytime. They are spots and blemishes, carousing in their own deceptions while they feast with you, having eyes full of adultery and that cannot cease from sin, enticing unstable souls. They have a heart trained in covetous practices, and are accursed children" (2 Peter 2:13–14).

James 4:4 says, "You adulterous people, don't you know that friendship with the world means enmity against God? Therefore, anyone who chooses to be a friend of the world becomes an enemy of God" (NIV). James calls people who flirt with the world adulterous. Peter also mentions spiritual adultery. "Having eyes full of adultery and that cannot cease from sin, enticing unstable souls. They have a heart trained in covetous practices, and are accursed children" (2 Peter 2:14).

Once again, these false prophets are covetous after the things of the world, and they promote all the riches, wealth, and luxury of this world. They promote these things to you. They say, "I will sit down with you and feast with you." You invite them to your church, listen to them, and give them donations. You give them finances, and you hope that their blessing over you will be a thirty, sixty, or hundredfold increase for you. "They have forsaken the right way and gone astray, following the way of Balaam the son of Beor, who loved the wages of unrighteousness; but he was rebuked for his iniquity: a dumb donkey speaking with a man's voice restrained the madness of the prophet" (2 Peter 2:15–16).

Balaam was a prophet who started to be a prophet for hire. He started to do prophecies for money. These prophets run their ministry to make money. They're doing everything possible to make a profit and live a lavish, covetous lifestyle. They tell you that it's okay for you to be rich.

It's okay for you to be rich, healthy, wealthy, wise, and prosperous in all your ways. They say, "Give us your money, and the Lord will bless you some thirty, some sixty, and some a hundredfold."

How do you avoid the false prophets and teachers? You learn what the narrow way is.

There are two books that will help you. The first one is *Intoxicated with Babylon* by Steve Gallagher. That book talks about how people in the Christian church are friends with the world and how to come out of that addiction to the world and how to stop being lukewarm. The next book is called *Standing Firm in the Great Apostasy* by Steve Gallagher. This book will help you come out of false teaching and false understandings.

I hope that you've been blessed by this. I hope that quite a few people read this book. If you enjoyed this and you learned something, I'd encourage you to repent, to put away those teachers, to get rid of those books and teachings, and to stop following the YouTube videos of false teachers and prophets that you've probably identified through my teaching.

They will be hard to let go of because you love them and follow them for a reason. They give you a message that's encouraging, uplifting, and nice to listen to. They flatter you. They'll be hard to let go of.

I encourage you to repent, to turn from your ways. Buy the two books I mentioned previously and start to walk on the narrow path. Download the article on "The Fifty Commands of Jesus."[9] Start to obey those commands. Not as practicing the law, not as a heavy burden on your heart, but as a proper way to love God and to love your fellow man. They are the instructions on how to do it.

If you like this book and you have some comments, please write a review on Amazon mentioning this chapter. Check out my internet site. Check out my other books. Write to me at my email address. Get in touch. Until we meet in heaven, God bless you.

CHAPTER 2:

Getting Real About Money and God

This section might be helpful to you if any of the following apply:

- you're a prosperity preacher who is reading this chapter,
- you have been taught by preachers that it's okay to be rich and wealthy, or
- you have been told that you can go and do all the great things in the world and have all the finest possessions in the world and be a Christian.

I'm reading a book called *Spiritual Avalanche* by Steve Hill. He made six points when it came to the defense against prosperity preaching.[10] The number one point is that Jesus warned against storing up treasures on earth.

Matthew 6:19–21 says, "Do not lay up for yourselves treasures on earth, where moth and rust destroy and where thieves break in and steal; but lay up for yourselves treasures in heaven, where neither moth nor rust destroy and where thieves do not break in and steal. For where your treasure is, there your heart will be also."

How do you store up this treasure in heaven? You can give toward ministries that are saving the lost. You can give toward ministries that are helping Christians become more passionate, more real, more authentic, and more effective in their faith. I have a couple of books, *Princess Diana Speaks from Heaven* and *Michael Jackson Speaks from Heaven*, that help the lost to come into salvation. I have between forty and fifty books that help Christians develop a deeper faith.

You could sow into my ministry and store up treasures. All these things store up treasures:

- giving a cup of water to someone who's thirsty,
- buying a meal for a homeless person on the street,
- giving money to a widow or a single mom in your church so that she can pay for her groceries,
- doing anything to feed people, or
- doing anything to help people better understand the gospel.

You don't store up treasure in heaven when you are buying a fashionable, expensive dress. That is storing up treasure on earth.

For example, my whole life is focused on kingdom treasure, on treasure in heaven. I can confess that you see heaven more when you're always laying up your treasure in heaven. I tell my mom and my friends, "Mom, I'm selfish in one way. I'm selfish for rewards in heaven. I store up many rewards there. I'm selfish for them."

Jesus continued in Matthew 6:24. He said, "No one can serve two masters; for either he will hate the one and love the other, or else he will be loyal to the one and despise the other. You cannot serve God and mammon." Mammon can mean money, but it can mean money and possessions as well. Many people try to serve God and money or mammon. Mega churches and all kinds of churches are filled with carnal Christians who are spending all they can on the riches of the world and the assets and the treasures in this world and singing praises to God at the same time. They're trying to serve God and serve their flesh at the same time.

They're singing praises to God about how great he is to them, but they spend most of their finances on themselves, not on the poor, the destitute, or ministries. But they spend all their money on treasures of the world. To repeat, Jesus tells us "do not store up your treasure on earth." He commands us, "but store up treasure in heaven."

I've written a book on this called *Living for Eternity*. I wrote that book about living your life for eternity. It's surprising. Not many people actually buy that book. It's one of my lowest sellers out of more than fifty books because it seems that not many Christians are very interested in storing up treasures for eternity. They're more excited about spending money on the things of this world.

The second point Steve Hill talked about is the warning that Jesus gave against covetousness.[11] Luke 12:15 says, "And He said to them, 'Take heed and beware of covetousness, for one's life does not consist in the abundance of the things he possesses.'"

Here we are. It doesn't matter who has the best car. It doesn't matter who has the most CDs or DVDs or the largest record collection. It doesn't matter if your iTunes storage has a thousand albums on it. It doesn't matter if you have the latest iPhone or Mac computer. Life does not consist in the abundance of your possessions!

Jesus warned against covetousness. Covetousness is simply keeping up with the Jones's or keeping up with your neighbors. It's having flashy, shiny, and bright things, everything that gives you a temporary high. That's what the world does.

It's flashy, shiny, bright, and sparkly. You buy it and get a high. You get this high from buying something, consuming something. As weeks or months go by, the high disappears, and like a junkie, like someone who's shooting a needle up their arm, you need another high. You need another fix. You go out to buy something new.

Apple amazingly continues to sell iPhones, some for as much as AUD 2,000. People amazingly have that kind of cash to buy the latest iPhone. Jesus said in the previous verse, "Take heed and beware of covetousness." In 1 Corinthians 6:9–10, Paul preaches that the covetous will not inherit the kingdom of heaven. Your love of the world can stop you from going to heaven. That's not taught a lot these days.

In fact, prosperity preachers preach the opposite. They preach that you can have all the best that the world offers and have the best of Jesus. Their lives prove and demonstrate it. They have all the best cars, the best jewelry, the best houses, private planes, and television ministries. They own everything. "And then I will declare to them, 'I never knew you; depart from Me, you who practice lawlessness!'" (Matthew 7:23). Covetousness is lawlessness.

Will they be in heaven? Will you be there when they are turned away from heaven and sent to hell for participating in a covetous lifestyle? Are you going to be there as one of their followers, or will you change your ways, turn around, and repent and walk the other way?

Jesus emphasized caring for the poor. Matthew 25:31–46 addresses this. Verses 41–46 say,

Then He will also say to those on the left hand, "Depart from Me, you cursed, into the everlasting fire prepared for the devil and his angels: for I was hungry and you gave Me no food; I was thirsty and you gave Me no drink; I was a stranger and you did not take Me in, naked and you did not clothe Me, sick and in prison and you did not visit Me."

Then they also will answer Him, saying, "Lord, when did we see You hungry or thirsty or a stranger or naked or sick or in prison, and did not minister to You?" Then He will answer them, saying, "Assuredly, I say to you, inasmuch as you did not do it to one of the least of these, you did not do it to Me." And these will go away into everlasting punishment, but the righteous into eternal life.

Jesus emphasized how to care for the poor. He wants you to care for those without anything to drink, which are the homeless. He wants you to care for those without food, the people in foreign nations as well as the poor in your own city. He wants you to care for those in your churches that are going without adequate food, possessions, and clothes. He wants us to care for people who are homeless, who need new clothes, who need a drink, and who need food. He wants us to reach out to the poor.

You can search under the word poor in Psalms and Proverbs. Many of these passages, mostly in the Psalms, tell you to care for the poor. If you do, the Lord will love you and pour out blessings upon your life.

We all know the parable of the sheep and the goats, but do you live it? If this parable stood for who was going to get into heaven, would you get into heaven? That's a serious question you have to ask yourself because the great majority of Christians that I have known wouldn't make it to heaven, according to this parable. These Christians walk past homeless people who have asked them for money. These people ignore the cries of those who are hungry and poor. It shouldn't be, but that's the case. It's a sad condition. Jesus told us to care for the poor.

The next point says that John taught that we should not live according to the present age.[12] I quote 1 John 2:15–17 often. You'll love this if you follow my books and teachings. You'll love how I share this verse so often. It's in so many of my books, and I like the *New Living Translation.* "Do not love this world nor the things it offers you, for when you love the world, you do not have the love of the Father in you. For the world offers only a craving for physical pleasure, a craving for everything we see, and pride in our achievements and possessions. These are not from the Father, but are from this world. And this world is fading away, along with everything that people crave. But anyone who does what pleases God will live forever."

If you don't have the love of the Father in you, are you a Christian? Who will live forever? The people who please God. What pleases God? Jesus said, "If anyone wants to come after me, he must deny himself, take up his cross, and follow me" (Matthew 16:24, author's paraphrase).

Deny himself.

Denying yourself is the opposite of living for the world, its lusts, and its pleasures. Denying yourself is spending $30 on an orphan overseas instead of buying a new DVD each month. It means going without in order to bless someone in ministry.

Do modern Christians even know how to go without? This is totally contrary to the prosperity messages that I hear preached by people. The Word says to go without and to deny yourself. John says here, "Do not love the world or the things that it offers you. For when you love the world, you do not have the love of the Father in you." Do you love the world? Do you love the world, the things of the world? Are you consumed by this world and its passions?

If you are, the Scripture points at the fact that you're not going to heaven. It says at the end, "But anyone who does what pleases God will live forever." What pleases God? Deny yourself and take up your cross and follow me, Jesus said.

Jesus wasn't walking around with lots of wealth and possessions. He didn't even have a change of clothes. One time, he was asked for money when he was with Peter, and he didn't have it. He had money with Judas in a money belt.

They used to have two lines when Jesus ministered, a line for healing and a line for money. Two types of people would come. The sick people would be healed by Jesus and the disciples. The people who needed alms, the people who were beggars, used to come to Judas, and Judas gave them money. Rich people, the wealthy, and those of ordinary means just kept coming to Jesus and giving him money. Jesus would give it to Judas.

Money was constantly coming in and going out. There's nothing wrong with having a ministry that generates $20 million dollars a week as long as the money is circulating and not buying $20 million and $50 million houses. I can't fathom why someone would have a $50 million house when there are churches in India with two hundred people meeting in a paddock out in the open on Sundays. They don't have their own church building or church land.

When I was in India fifteen years ago, it only cost about $7,000 to buy the land and build a building. For $7,000, two hundred Christians could be fed the word of the Lord in any sort of weather condition. But some Christians drive down the road in $250,000 cars and think they're being blessed by the Lord. A $250,000 car is like thirty churches that could be built and six thousand Christians could be blessed with their own church home in a hostile Hindu country.

The next point from Steve Hill is that Jesus did not die to make us financially wealthy but to save us from our sins.[13] The verse quoted is Matthew 1:21. "And she will bring forth a Son, and you shall call His name Jesus, for He will save His people from their sins." That's why Jesus came.

Jesus didn't come to make us financially wealthy or blessed. Jesus came to save us from our sin. One of the main sins in the modern world, in the Christian church today, is this love of the world, this covetousness, this going after the things of the world and being possessed by a zeal for and the love of the things of the world.

It has to stop. It has to stop in your life. You have to turn around because you won't find a lot of wealthy, rich people in heaven. Jesus used an exaggeration when he said it's easier for a camel to pass through the eye of the needle than for a rich man to get to heaven. (See Matthew 19:24.) When Jesus said this, he was speaking in hyperbole. Hyperbole is an overstated exaggeration used to make a point. An example today would be when a mom tells her child, "If I've told you once, I've told you a million times, take out the trash!" The child knows that the mom doesn't literally mean "a million times." The mom is using hyperbole to drive home the point.

Jesus was doing the same thing here. Yes, a rich man can get into heaven. It is possible for a rich person to get to heaven, but it's very difficult. The rich often put more value on their wealth than on following Jesus. Paul says, "We all came into the world with nothing. We'll all leave without anything. With food and clothing, we should be content" (1 Timothy 6:7–8, author's paraphrase). Paul was hinting at the fact that you have to be stripped of everything to enter heaven.

Does that mean the rich can't get to heaven? Certainly not! Wealthy people who give a tremendous amount to the kingdom of God and invest in Christians and the work of the ministry can definitely go to heaven. But it's hard for a rich person to give up their wealth and go without the things that wealth can buy them.

James, Jesus's brother, says in James 2:5, "Listen, my beloved brethren: Has God not chosen the poor of this world to be rich in faith and heirs of the kingdom which He promised to those who love Him?"

James was saying quite clearly there that it's easy for the poor to be blessed and rich in faith. When you're poor, that's all you have. But you can still be covetous as a poor person. Many people don't have a lot of wealth, but they have zeal and a hunger for wealth. Many people who don't have a lot of money spend money on lottery tickets because they think that if they win the lottery, it'll solve all their problems. Many Bible-believing Christians buy these tickets, thinking that God will choose this way to bless them.

People gamble for those reasons. Poor people can spend a dollar on a scratch-it ticket or a lotto ticket, hoping to get rich and climb out of their poverty. Rich people aren't the only ones who can be bound up with covetousness.

What I found really disgusting when I was homeless for a time is that homeless people steal from each other. You think that your situation is pretty bad when you're homeless, but you can't leave a cell phone lying around in a homeless hostel.

You can't put a cell phone into a power socket to charge and leave it there and walk away. You have to be sitting next to your phone for the hour while it charges because if you leave it unattended, an addict or alcoholic will steal your phone and take it to a secondhand store and sell it.

Here's a message for you prosperity teachers. I want you to listen up. All of you people who are caught up and bound with riches, wealth, and spending, Jesus can bless you.

I want to share something. Last year, my ministry spent $46,000 producing books. I received $20,000 from the government on a disability pension that I lived on and used to pay my rent, food, and other bills. I received $46,000 through my ministry by giving personal prophecies and from donations from people. But I spent $46,000 producing books.

I could have spent $46,000 on myself and bought a lovely car and some really flashy clothes. But I spent it on producing books that I practically give away for ninety-nine cents. What are you doing with your money? Are you storing up treasures in heaven? Do you know how to store up treasures in heaven?

My book *Living for Eternity* would probably help you. I encourage you to buy the audiobook or the paperback. (It's not presently available as an e-book.) I'd encourage you to buy and listen to this audiobook or read the paperback.

Just grab this book and let it transform your life so that you start living a life to build up treasure in heaven. A $50 million house and a Porsche won't help you if you're sent to hell. You'd want to trade everything you earned financially, all your possessions, to escape hell. You'd trade everything for one minute outside the flames of hell.

It's serious. Prosperity teaching is a false teaching. It's taking people to hell because of the sin of covetousness. If you don't know you're coveting, you can't repent. I'm hoping that the messages in the time I spend sharing with you will penetrate your hearts so that you decide to repent, change your ways, and take a serious look at your life.

I hope that this has touched you and affected you for the better. You can comment on Amazon if this has blessed you.

CHAPTER 3:

Storing up a Good Foundation

The apostle Paul spoke about money in his letter to Timothy. We all know the famous verse that he shared. As I mentioned in the previous chapter, 1 Timothy 6:6–11 says, Now godliness with contentment is great gain. For we brought nothing into this world, and it is certain we can carry nothing out. And having food and clothing, with these we shall be content. But those who desire to be rich fall into temptation and a snare, and into many foolish and harmful lusts which drown men in destruction and perdition. For the love of money is a root of all kinds of evil, for which some have strayed from the faith in their greediness, and pierced themselves through with many sorrows.

But you, O man of God, flee these things and pursue righteousness, godliness, faith, love, patience, gentleness.

There is a lot of wisdom in that passage. With food and clothing, you should be content. Judas was said to be the man of perdition. Perdition means losing your salvation or going to a place where your salvation doesn't save you anymore. It's serious stuff. This passage talks about drowning. You can survive if you almost drown. But when you drown, you die. Paul is talking about a spiritual death here.

Paul then addresses people who have strayed from the faith. That means they departed the faith. Through the love of money, they departed the faith. They've drowned in perdition. This is serious stuff.

How can we be wealthy and persevere? How can we survive if we're wealthy? If you remember, Jesus said it's hard for a rich man to go to heaven, to inherit heaven. It's easier for a camel to go through the eye of a needle as I said earlier. Jesus spoke in hyperbole to make a point about how difficult it is for a rich person to go to heaven.

Paul then says to flee these things. Flee wanting to be rich and instead pursue righteousness, godliness, faith, love, patience, and gentleness.

It seems that money can take you out of the kingdom. In Proverbs 30:8–9, Solomon says, "Give me neither poverty nor riches—feed me with the food allotted to me; lest I be full and deny You, and say, 'Who is the Lord?' Or lest I be poor and steal, and profane the name of my God." His words in Proverbs are wise. He understood that if he were in lack, he'd curse the Lord. Yet he knew if he had too much, he'd depart from the Lord.

The problem with the modern age is that we have a lot of wealth. Paul would even consider someone on a pension, even someone on government assistance in America, as living better than people that were kings in the past. They have flushing toilets, microwaves, DVDs, computers, iPhones, and all the modern conveniences. They're on government assistance. Don't consider for one moment that you're not rich. This isn't talking about billionaires.

"But those who desire to be rich fall into temptation and a snare, and into many foolish and harmful lusts which drown men in destruction and perdition." He goes onto say that "The love of money is the root of all kinds of evil for which some have strayed from the faith in their greediness and pierced themselves through with many sorrows."

There is a clear warning from Paul. Don't pursue riches. It's okay to have wealth. Some men and women of God are really blessed in business, and they give to the Lord and finance the Lord's kingdom. Some people manage money really well. Before they were wealthy, they were giving away 50 percent of what they earned. When they became billionaires, they were giving away 90 percent of their income. They're the kinds of people the Lord loves.

But so many people want the riches of the wicked stored up for the righteous. So many people hear that preached and want to be millionaires. They say that they want to be millionaires so that they can share with other people, but they're not currently giving 30 percent of their income when they're poor. They're not even giving 10 percent.

So many people want wealth but not because of the Lord or to sow more into kingdom. Here was the apostle Paul, one of the greatest apostles, who wrote one-third of the New Testament, saying these things. He built and made tents for rich people to finance his ministry. He worked full-time and then ministered part-time. He spoke on money often, and we should pay attention to him.

How does the apostle Paul suggest that we store up a good foundation for ourselves? How does he suggest that wealthy and rich people operate? He says in 1 Timothy 6:17, "Command those who are rich in this present age not to be haughty, nor to trust in uncertain riches but in the living God, who gives us richly all things to enjoy."

First of all, don't be proud and don't trust in uncertain riches.

He says, "But we should trust in the living God who gives to us richly all things to enjoy."

First, don't be proud. Second, don't trust in uncertain riches that can be here today and gone tomorrow. But trust the living God that gives to us richly.

"Let them do good, that they be rich in good works, ready to give, willing to share" (1 Timothy 6:18).

If you even receive a disability pension, you should be following this verse. We in the West are rich compared to most of the world that lives on two dollars a day.

What are we in the West to do as rich people? We're to be rich in good works, ready to give, and willing to share. That's what we're to do. That's how we build up a good foundation, storing up for ourselves a good foundation for the time to come that we may lay hold of eternal life.

The apostle Paul here tells us how to store up a good foundation. He's saying we should be ready to give and willing to share. I quoted before that we are to bless other people. We're to be used to share our money, to give money, to support other people, to support those who are not as wealthy as ourselves, to be willing to give, willing to share, and to be a blessing to people. That's how we store up a good foundation.

Only if you're doing those things—only if you are sharing, giving, and blessing other people before you become wealthy—will you continue to give when you're wealthy. If you were earning $1,000 every two weeks with your income and you're giving $300 of that $1,000 to needy people and to the Lord and ministries, when you're earning $1 million a week, would you give away $300,000 or would you give away $500,000? You need to develop a habit.

I have read that the wealthier the Christians are in the United States, the smaller percentage of their income they give to the Lord. So just because you suddenly become wealthy does not mean that you will always be a big giver. You need to start to give now.

Recently I learned of a person who was involved with my ministry who was coming into a lot of money. It took self-control not to ask, "Hey, what about me?" You would be surprised how many wealthy people are asked for money from people in need. Just think of all the people overseas that try and friend request you on Facebook just to ask for money.

Do you understand this message? We need to be willing to share, ready to give, and use those attributes to store up a good foundation for ourselves. It's very dangerous when you move into a place where you have a lot of money. The people in the West go to doctors for prescriptions instead of going to God for their needs. The richer we become in the West, the more lukewarm we are and the less we think we need God.

Over in Africa, where people have no money, they really need God. Those people become sick, and their only chance is to be healed by God. In first-world countries, we go to the doctor. We take a pill to fix that sickness. We get a headache and reach for medication rather than laying our hands on our head and praying for healing of the headache.

I want to smile. I want to smile at you and wink and say God bless you. But that's the way to build up a good foundation: by giving. Giving is the way. That's the way to store up a good foundation, not hoarding and keeping it to yourself and getting all the best that the world can offer.

I hope that this has been helpful for you. I hope that you have listened to my words and the words from the apostle Paul, who was very knowledgeable and who impacted millions of people throughout the centuries with what he wrote in the Bible. I encourage you to consider obeying what he told Timothy to do. May God bless you and keep you. If you have any comments, please write a review. (By the way, in each video from which this book was made, I ask for comments on the YouTube video. I am just changing that in the book and asking people to write a review.)

I want to share the big admission of this YouTube video with you, which is right at the end. If you watched until the end, you'd see it. I don't know many things. But as a teacher, I always have an open mind so that I can find answers to my questions. I have hundreds of questions. There are many things that I don't know, and I mostly teach only on what I know. God bless.

CHAPTER 4:

Can We Love the World and Still Go to Heaven?

This is an important question. I have some Scriptures to share here instead of just sharing from my heart as I normally do. I chose some passages from the Word for this section.

We know that Jesus speaks in the book of Revelation. In Revelation 3:14–17, he says, "And to the angel of the church of the Laodiceans write, 'These things says the Amen, the Faithful and True Witness, the Beginning of the creation of God: "I know your works, that you are neither cold nor hot. I could wish you were cold or hot. So then, because you are lukewarm, and neither cold nor hot, I will vomit you out of My mouth. Because you say, 'I am rich, have become wealthy, and have need of nothing'—and do not know that you are wretched, miserable, poor, blind, and naked."'"

My question to people when I share this is, if Jesus is going vomit these lukewarm people out of his mouth, is he going to come back and pick up all his vomit and put it back into his mouth? Would you do that? Have you ever been sick and vomited? You wouldn't say to yourself, "Oh no, that's part of me. I can't lose part of me. That's yesterday's dinner. I'd better pick that up and put it back into my system." Do you ever pick up your vomit and put it back?

If you are lukewarm, if you say that you're rich and wealthy and have need of nothing, if you're lukewarm, do you think Jesus will put you back into his mouth when he vomits you out? I don't think so. I think that when you vomit, it's because you want to get rid of something, something that's annoying.

If you get hot coffee and leave it for a while, it becomes lukewarm and is not very palatable. The same thing happens if you heat up a meal and you don't leave it in the microwave long enough. The meal comes out and is lukewarm, and you can't eat it. You can eat a hot meal or a cold meal, but it's really difficult and nauseating to try to eat a lukewarm meal.

I want you to consider that Scripture. Are you in love with the world? The second scripture might make the point more completely. As I said in a previous chapter, this passage is found in 1 John 2:15–17 (NLT).

"Do not love this world nor the things it offers you, for when you love the world, you do not have the love of the Father in you. For the world offers only a craving for physical pleasure, a craving for everything we see, and pride in our achievements and possessions. These are not from the Father, but are from this world. And this world is fading away, along with everything that people crave. But anyone who does what pleases God will live forever."

The passage states, "but anyone who does what pleases God will live forever." From that, we can infer that people who don't do what pleases God won't live forever in heaven. Everyone has a choice of living forever. Their destination is what's in question. Are you living in the world and coveting the things of the world? Are you looking at what other people earn, what they drive, and the houses and clothes they have? Do you find yourself coveting? Do you have a lifestyle of coveting what your neighbor has, what others have? Do you find yourself wanting the same things for yourself?

That's being covetous and is a practice of sin. If it's not repented of with changed behavior, you can't be forgiven of that. You can only really be forgiven from sins that you turn away from and repent of.

Let's look at another passage, James 4:2–4.

You want what you don't have, so you scheme and kill to get it. You are jealous of what others have, but you can't get it, so you fight and wage war to take it away from them. Yet you don't have what you want because you don't ask God for it. And even when you ask, you don't get it because your motives are all wrong—you want only what will give you pleasure.

You adulterers! Don't you realize that friendship with the world makes you an enemy of God? I say it again: If you want to be a friend of the world, you make yourself an enemy of God (NLT).

The question I ask when people have read that Scripture in my books is how many of God's enemies are going to heaven? You might decide to be a friend of the world and consume everything in the world and not take up your cross and deny yourself. You might live your life in church on Sunday, but from Monday to Saturday, you live in the world and consume all the things of the world. If that's you, then how does this passage show you that lifestyle is wrong? If there is no difference between your spending habits and those of a non-Christian, are you really in love with Jesus? Or do you have the same love for the world and its ways as the non-Christian does?

If you live this covetous lifestyle and buy one good or service that's advertised to you after another, what makes you any different from the world? What makes you stand out? If you're a friend of the world and continue to be a friend of the world, what will you do if you're an enemy of God? If you are an enemy of God and don't change how you live and don't repent or change your lifestyle, then you remain an enemy of God. You might be watching or reading this and not even be aware that you're an enemy of God. The modern church doesn't teach this, and it's a difficult subject. I don't like to teach this. A lot prosperity-preaching churches say that you can have the best the world offers you and be a Christian. The more of the world that's in you, the less the Holy Spirit can fill your life, the less oil that is in your lamp when you live a life that is full of the world.

Do you think if you never change your ways, if you maintain a covetous lifestyle as a friend of the world, that God would accept you into heaven because you didn't know better? I certainly know that if you read this book and don't repent but remain in that lifestyle, you won't have a good end.

In Matthew 13, Jesus spoke of the sower and the three seeds that didn't grow. One of the seeds fell among the thorns, and the thorns choked it out. The *New Living Translation* says this in verse 22: "The seed that fell among the thorns represents those that heed the word, but all too quickly, the message is crowded out by the worries of this life and the lure of wealth. No fruit is produced."

The *New King James* says, "Now he who received seed among the thorns is he who hears the word, and the cares of this world and the deceitfulness of riches choke the word, and he becomes unfruitful."

Riches are deceitful. They'll lie to you. Living in this world and being a part of this world is dangerous for a Christian. It's wrong to live as a covetous Christian, a Christian who pursues after the things of the world advertised to them. They see someone on television advertising certain products and saying they are fantastic. The ad raves about a nice dress or the current fashions. They go after the things of the world rather than going after God.

That Scripture about the thorns choking out the Word with weeds is Matthew 13:22. In 1 Corinthians 6:9–10, Paul says, "Do you not know that the unrighteous will not inherit the kingdom of God? Do not be deceived. Neither fornicators, nor idolaters, nor adulterers, nor homosexuals, nor sodomites, nor thieves, nor covetous, nor drunkards, nor revilers, nor extortioners will inherit the kingdom of God."

Isn't it interesting that Paul says, "Do not be deceived?" This passage makes it sound as if people will bring in teachings that teach the opposite of what he's teaching. He says that neither fornicators [people who are having sex outside of marriage] or idolaters [people who make a god out of something] will inherit the kingdom of God. Idolaters can also be covetous people. Paul specifically says, "Neither fornicators, nor idolaters, nor adulterers, nor homosexuals, nor sodomites, nor thieves, nor covetous, nor drunkards, nor revilers, nor extortioners will inherit the kingdom of God."

Idolaters are those who are making a god out of something, those who have put something else in the place of God, which you can do when you're living in the world. Covetous people are constantly going after what other people have, and they are also practicing idolatry. Those people won't inherit the kingdom of God.

Can we love the world and still go to heaven? No, we can't! We need to turn around our behavior. Turn around the way we live and do something different.

I have read a book, *Intoxicated with Babylon* by Steve Gallagher, that will explain this more and that goes into a lot more depth on this subject. I encourage you to spend your precious money and purchase a copy of that book. The whole book addresses the effects of the spirit of the age, the effect that the spirit of this world has on Christians and how to come out of that deception that the enemy brings to the body of Christ.

I don't bring this message in pride or in a posture of condemnation. I bring this message because I don't live in the world. I've removed myself from the world. I'm in the world but not of it. I want others to turn around and change their behavior because according to my Scriptures, according to the verses I have just shared, the faith of people is hanging in the balance. God bless you.

CHAPTER 5:

Can a Rich Man Enter Heaven?

The apostle Paul in Timothy commands the rich not to be haughty or proud but to be generous and willing to share and give. The rich should not be haughty and trust uncertain riches but place their trust in the living God who gives to us liberally. You need to remove pride. You need to remove everything that is part of your life that keeps you from God, including possessions.

This reminds me of when Jesus spoke to the rich young ruler. He says the same words to us too. Jesus said, "One thing you lack: Go your way, sell whatever you have and give to the poor, and you will have treasure in heaven; and come, take up the cross, and follow Me" (Mark 10:21). Jesus didn't have a whole camel full of possessions; he didn't even have a change of clothes. He instructed his disciples to go out, teach, preach, do miracles, and not even take a moneybag or a change of clothes.

Remember the expression about the camel going through the eye of the needle. It's possible, but it takes humility along with a concerted effort. Rich people can get to heaven. Jesus wasn't saying that a rich person couldn't get to heaven. But they have to make entering heaven a goal.

I once met an evangelist who met the Queen of England. The queen invited him to the palace. He had a reputation for preaching the gospel on the streets of London. He was on the news and well-known. They discussed some pleasantries before the queen got down to business. She said, "I'm concerned about all my wealth. If I'm going to make it to heaven, do I need to give more? Do I need to do more charity? I want to be sure of my salvation."

These are the words of a person who's planning to go to heaven. She understood that she needed to make an intentional effort to overcome this serious obstacle and "get a camel through the eye of the needle" in Jesus's words. She had to focus on what she needed to do: following Jesus. Her wealth couldn't distract her from this goal. She had to use her wealth in a godly way and make specific plans to spend her money to glorify God. Her priorities needed to change; she couldn't just waste money buying expensive clothes, eating at luxurious restaurants, driving the best cars, or spending her wealth on frivolous things.

While we look at this example and think these words of Jesus might not apply to us, you might be surprised to find that they are relevant today. Nearly 50 percent of the world's population lives on less than $2.50 a day.[14] I'm on a disability pension from my government, and I would still be considered rich, according to these standards. I have even heard it said that the cats in America live better than one-third of the world's population.

We're considered rich. We have to plan to go to heaven. As I shared before, can we love the world and still go to heaven? You have to ask yourself: What do the Scriptures teach about loving the world and being part of the world?

It's a lot more difficult to go to heaven than many preachers preach. You have to make a concerted effort to make sure that you aren't living an idolatrous or covetous life. A rich person can go to heaven, but not the type of rich person that most people in the West are, not the lukewarm Christian.

Closing Thoughts

I started to edit this book with a heavy heart but a heart full of hope for the readers. With over fifty books to my name, I know that a lot of people read nearly every book that I produce. I know that no matter the title of this book, some of my fans will read it. I write it for them because through my books, I feel that I have earned the right to speak to them.

The church is in the last days. Big name preachers are preaching the prosperity gospel and living unashamed in a blatantly covetous lifestyle. Their wealth, their assets, and the smiles on their faces are all there to convince you *that you can serve* both *God and money*. Even though they make the life look desirable, it is wickedness. I know it might help you if I listed twenty or so of these names for you, but I promised myself and God never to speak out against another minister by name. If you are following anyone that promotes getting rich, do what Paul says: Flee from that teacher and his/her ways and leave their teachings behind.

Another type of teacher teaches what is called hyper-grace. This type of grace speaks a lot about the finished works of Christ and says that any effort to secure your salvation is wrong. They teach that you believe error if you are trying to obey God to earn your way to heaven. They teach that you don't need to repent each time you sin; they teach that making an effort to be holy and righteous is wrong. These people teach that you don't have to obey Jesus and what he taught. This type of teacher needs a whole book to cover all the errors that they teach. Once again, speakers with big platforms and well-known preachers teach this message. A book that argues against this and that will give you more information on what teachings to steer clear of is *Hyper Grace: Exposing the Dangers of the Modern Hyper Grace Message* by Michael L. Brown. In that book, he names some of these teachers and has quotes from some who teach this message.

I hope that this message has convicted you, taught you something, and led you to change. I have a burden on my heart to warn every believer to leave their life of sin and pursue a life of holiness. I hope this simple message has not offended you too much. I will pray for you.

God bless.

Matthew Robert Payne
March 2019

I'd Love to Hear from You

One of the ways that you can bless me as a writer is by writing an honest and candid review of my book on the platform from which you purchased it. I always read the reviews of my books, and I would love to hear what you have to say about this one.

Before I buy a book, I read the reviews first. You can make an informed decision about a book when you have read enough honest reviews from readers. One way to help me sell this book and to give me positive feedback is by writing a review for me. It doesn't cost you a thing but helps me and the future readers of this book enormously.

To read my blog, request a life-coaching session, request your own personal prophecy, or receive a personal message from your angel, you can also visit my website at http://personal-prophecy-today.com. All of the funds raised through my ministry website will go toward the books that I write and self-publish.

To write to me about this book or to share any other thoughts, please feel free to contact me at my personal email address at survivors.sanctuary@gmail.com.

You can also friend request me on Facebook at Matthew Robert Payne. Please send me a message if we have no friends in common, as a lot of scammers now send me friend requests. As of November 2018, I'm starting an online church community via Zoom conferencing software, and I invite you to contact me to become part of this church.

You can also do me a huge favor and share this book on Facebook as a recommended book to read. This will help me and other readers.

How to Sponsor a Book Project

If you have been blessed by this book, you might consider sponsoring a book for me. It normally costs me at least $1,500—often more—to produce each book that I write, depending on the length of the book.

If you seek the Holy Spirit about financing a book for me, I know that the Lord would be eternally grateful to you. Consider how much this book has blessed you, and then think of hundreds or even thousands of people who would be blessed by a book of mine. As you are probably aware, the vast majority of my e-books are ninety-nine cents, which proves to you that book writing is indeed a ministry for me and not a money-making venture. I would be very happy if you supported me in this.

If you have any questions for me or if you want to know what projects I am currently working on that your money might finance, you can write to me at survivors.sanctuary@gmail.com and ask me for more information. I would be pleased to give you additional details about my projects.

You can sow any amount into my ministry by simply sending me money via the PayPal link at this address: http://personal-prophecy-today.com/support-my-ministry.

You can be sure that your support, no matter the amount, will be used for the publishing of helpful Christian books for people to read.

Further Reading

Intoxicated with Babylon by Steve Gallagher

Standing Firm through the Great Apostasy by Steve Gallagher

Hyper Grace: Exposing the Dangers of the Modern Hyper Grace Message by Michael L. Brown

If you want to read all about me and see my books, see www.amazon.com/author/matthewrobertpayne.

Acknowledgments

Jesus:

I want to thank you for being my lifelong friend and for never deserting me, no matter how dark my life became. You led me into some great adventures with saints and helped me put together this book.

Holy Spirit:

I want to thank you for leading and teaching me. You are a great teacher, better than I could ever be. You have been with me every step of the way. You had a lot to do with this book of mine, and I am thankful for that help. I hope I wasn't too tough on the readers.

Father:

Thank you for loving me and entrusting me with this life that I am living. Thank you for revealing my purpose to me and leading me toward accomplishing it. Thank you so much for your Son, Jesus. Thank you for everything that you have done in my life. Thank you for persevering with me.

Lisa Thompson:

Thank you, Lisa, for editing this book of mine. You take my simple words and transform them to make me seem smarter than I really am. *If you have any editing needs, contact Lisa at* writebylisa@gmail.com.

Alison Treat:

Thank you, Alison, for proofreading this book for me. I'm glad you're part of my team.

Friends:

Thank you, Darla, Lisa, Nicola, Mary, Laura, David Joseph, and Michael Van Vlymen for your friendship and for how you have impacted my life.

Mom and Dad:

Thank you, Mom and Dad, for all the love that you have given me. I am a product of your love.

Readers and ministry supporters:

Thank you, dear readers. Thank you, ministry supporters, for the funds that you have given me to publish books. I live to educate people, and I thank my readers and the supporters of my ministry because you make life worth living.

About Matthew Robert Payne

Matthew Robert Payne, a teacher and prophet, enjoys writing what the Lord puts on his heart to share. He receives great pleasure from interacting with others on Facebook, hearing from people who have read his books, and prophesying over people's lives. He is a passionate lover of and disciple of Jesus Christ. He hopes that as you discover his books, you will intimately come to know Jesus, the Father, and Matthew through his transparent writing style.

Matthew grew up in a traditional Baptist church and gave his heart to Jesus Christ at the tender age of eight years old. But he left home at the age of eighteen, living a wild life for many years and engaging in bad habits and addictions. At twenty-seven, he was baptized in water and, at the same time, baptized in the Holy Spirit. Matthew learned about the five-fold ministry offices and received a revelation of their value today.

He started his journey as a prophet twenty years ago, learning about this gift and putting it into practice. With thousands of prophecies under his belt, he can confidently prophesy to friends and strangers alike. He has been writing for a number of years and self-published his first book in 2011. Today he spends his time earning money to self-publish and writes a new book approximately every month. You can also find any of his sixteen hundred videos on YouTube on his channel under Matthew Robert Payne.

You can connect with him on Facebook. You can sow into his book-writing ministry, read his blog, receive a message from your angel, or even receive your own nine-minute personal prophecy from Matthew at http://personal-prophecy-today.com.

Blurb

Jesus warned in Matthew 24 that in the last days, many false prophets and teachers would arise who would lead many astray. He said even the elect of God might be deceived if that were possible. We can see from the rest of Matthew 24 that we are clearly approaching these times. So where are the false prophets, and is what we are being taught by popular teachers leading us into deception?

For twenty years, Matthew Robert Payne struggled to find the answers to these perplexing questions: Who are these people; are they Christians, and what did they do to deserve Jesus's harsh words? In this short book, you can find the answers to these questions.

Join Matthew as he pleads with you to see the truth of the Gospels as taught by Jesus, Paul, Peter, and James. You will learn how you can turn from the false teachings that you have heard and live righteously so that you can be assured of eternal life.

---

[1] "The Narrow Way, Matthew 7:13–14," *New King James Version*, Bible Gateway, accessed March 27, 2019, https://www.biblegateway.com/passage/?search=Matthew+7%3A13-14&version=NKJV.

[2] "Strong's #3045, *yada*," *Greek and Hebrew Definitions*, Bible Tools, accessed March 27, 2019, https://www.bibletools.org/index.cfm/fuseaction/Lexicon.show/ID/H3045/yada%60.htm.

3 "Build on the Rock, Matthew 7:24–29," *New King James Version*, Bible Gateway, accessed March 27, 2019, https://www.biblegateway.com/passage/?search=Matthew+7%3A24-29&version=NKJV.

4 Matthew Robert Payne, "The Fifty Commands of Jesus," *Ezine*, February 26, 2007, http://ezinearticles.com/?The-Fifty-Commands-of-Jesus&id=468177.

5 Ibid.

6 "Destructive Doctrines, 2 Peter 2:1–3," *New King James Version*, Bible Gateway, accessed March 27, 2019, https://www.biblegateway.com/passage/?search=2+peter+2%3A1-9&version=NKJV.

7 "Doom of False Teachers, 2 Peter 2:4–9," New King James Version, Bible Gateway, accessed March 27, 2019, https://www.biblegateway.com/passage/?search=2+peter+2%3A1-9&version=NKJV.

8 "Depravity of False Teachers, 2 Peter 2:12–17," New King James Version, Bible Gateway, accessed March 27, 2019, https://www.biblegateway.com/passage/?search=2+peter+2%3A10-20&version=NKJV.

9 Payne, "The Fifty Commands of Jesus," *Ezine*.

10 Steve Hill, *Spiritual Avalanche: The Threat of False Teachings that Could Destroy Millions*, (Florida: Charisma House, 2013), www.amzn.com/B00B6TV0K8.

11 Ibid.

12 Ibid.

13 Ibid.

14 "Poverty Facts and Stats," *Global Issues* , last updated January 7, 2013, http://www.globalissues.org/article/26/poverty-facts-and-stats.

www.ingramcontent.com/pod-product-compliance
Lightning Source LLC
Chambersburg PA
CBHW021941040426